What Do Yo Like?

Written by Phillipe Bernard

Illustrated by Hayal Aydin

Short *i* (CVC words)		**Long *i* (VCe words)**	
big	gift	bride	Mike
bin	pigs	fine	ride
fins		hide	time
		like	

High-Frequency Words

funny	some	were	you
one	they	what	

1

What do you like?

I like the funny one.
The bride bakes a cake.
The cake is not fine.

What do you like?
I like this one.

Some men ride to help.
They were in time.

What do you like?
I like the one with the pigs.

Mike and Ben are pigs.
Mike and Ben hide in a big bin.
It is funny.

What do you like?
I like the gift with fins!